AND OTHER GREAT POEMS BY
GABRIEL FITZMAURICE

D1637876

To John and Nessa,
as it was in the beginning

ILLUSTRATED BY
STELLA MACDONALD & NiCKY PHELAN

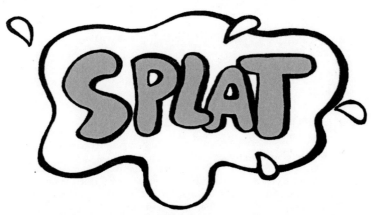

AND OTHER GREAT POEMS BY
GABRIEL FiTZMAURICE

MERCIER PRESS
IRISH PUBLISHER – IRISH STORY

MERCIER PRESS
www.mercierpress.ie
Cork

© Text: Gabriel Fitzmaurice, 2012
© Illustrations: Nicky Phelan and Stella Macdonald, 2012

978 1 85635 953 5

10 9 8 7 6 5 4 3 2 1

A CIP record for this title is available from the British Library

Printed and bound in the EU

Contents

Introduction

Hello everybody!

I hope you enjoy reading these poems as much as I enjoyed writing them. This collection contains poems from all my books for the young and young at heart – many of them long out of print. For me it is like visiting old friends. For some of you it will be, too. For others who are new to my work I hope it will be like making new friends.

People come up to me in schools, in hotels, in pubs, in theatres and on the street and tell me how much they have enjoyed my poems. In writing them I have drawn from my experience of being a primary school teacher for thirty-five years. The children I taught were an inspiration and a challenge that I miss now that I have retired from the classroom. I have also been inspired to write by my two children, John and Nessa, now both grown up. Indeed Nessa is now a mammy herself – to Katie Margaret Crowley, who has started me writing again, this time as a doting grandad. I also include poems about my own childhood. Everybody tells me I was a very cross child and this translated itself into a somewhat subversive adulthood that sometimes sees the world upside down, and a very good place it is too!

Here are serious poems and silly poems, sad poems and happy poems, naughty poems and nice poems that celebrate our eternal youth. If you can't laugh or cry at these poems, you're OLD! As Bob Dylan sang: 'May you be forever young'. God bless.

Gabriel Fitzmaurice

A Cross Boy

I'm a cross boy. I can't help it.
I get into trouble each day –
In trouble at home, in trouble at school
For the things that I do and I say.

Then I thought of a plan to get better,
To keep me from trouble, and so
I opened my mam's holy water
And drank the whole lot in one go.

I drank all my mam's holy water
She'd brought in a bottle from Lourdes,
I drank all my mam's holy water
Hoping that I would get cured.

But no! I'm as crazy as ever,
My plan didn't work. Never could.
I thought I'd get better by magic
But it takes more than that to get good.

I'm a cross boy. I can't help it.
I get into trouble here still
But even cross boys can do better.
I can try to do better. I will.

The Teacher

I kinda like the teacher
But he's most awful cross,
He really throws his weight about,
He sure can act the boss.

But still, he tells us stories
And he's nice and funny too,
He's nice – but he could be nicer.
I suppose we could be nicer too.

Spider

Hairy spider on the wall!
John stiffens, John bawls;

Cool as you like while John fretted,
Nessa picked it up and ate it.

An Apple for the Teacher

'Bring apples to eat,' the teacher said,
But me, I'd rather mush
So I threw mine down the toilet
But the apple wouldn't flush.

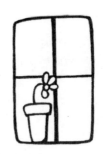

It just kept bobbing like a ball
As the flush foamed all about,
So I put my hand in the toilet bowl
And took the apple out.

I washed it in the basin
So nobody would know
Then dried it on my jumper
And gave it to 'Mister O'

(That's what we call our teacher),
He rubbed it once or twice
And then he ate my apple.
He said 'twas very nice.

Belly Buttons

An 'inny' or an 'outie' –
A belly button goes
In like Dingle Harbour
Or out like the Pope's Nose.

An 'inny' or an 'outie' –
What kind of one have you?
I wish I had an 'inny'
'Cos mine sticks out. Boo hoo!

Santa Claus

Santa Claus is coming
To the village hall,
I'm going to see Santa Claus
And I won't cry at all.

Hello Santa! This is me!
(Oh Dad, he's awful hairy!
Oh Dad, don't let him near me!
Oh Dad, he's awful scary!).

Santa Claus was here today
In the village hall –
He gave me crisps and lemonade
(All I could do was bawl).

My Hurley

Left! Right! Left! Right!
Marching down the hall,
My hurley as a rifle.
About turn at the wall.

I'm a soldier, Mammy.
(A hurley's best by far –
Today it can be a gun,
Tomorrow a guitar).

Beebla

For John and Nessa

Beebla wasn't sure that he was born
(What was it to be born? He didn't know),
But his mother had been dying four or five times:
Beebla threatened God: 'Don't let her go –
If You do, then I won't say my prayers;
If You do, then I won't go to Mass.'
The priest came and anointed Beebla's Mammy.
Next morning, Beebla boasted in his class:
'My mother was anointed in the night-time;
The priest came to our house, I stayed up late.'
Beebla was cock-proud of his achievement:
All the class was listening – this was great!

Beebla played with all the boys at playtime
(The girls were in the school across the way) –
They played football with a sock stuffed with old
    papers,
He'd forget about his Mammy in the play.
But always at the back of all his playing,
He knew about anointing in the night,

L209, 210/

And, knowing this, there could be no un-knowing –
Nothing in the world would change that quite.

Beebla got a motor-car in London –
A blue one with pedals which he craved
(Beebla'd been in hospital in London,
And, coming home, he'd had to have his way);
So his Daddy bought him his blue motor-car,
He drove it all the way out to the 'plane,
And touching down, cranky with excitement,
He squealed till he was in his car again.

He drove around the village, a born show-off;
He pulled into a funeral, kept his place,
And all the funeral cars, backed up behind him,
Couldn't hoot, for that would be disgrace!
He drove off from the Chapel to the graveyard,
And, tiring, he pulled out and headed back;
When his mother heard about it, she went purple
And grabbed for her *wallop-spoon* to smack;

But his Daddy shielded Beebla from her wallops –
They brushed across his Daddy's legs until
His mother's rage fizzled to a token:
She shook the spoon, and threatened that she'd kill
Him if he didn't mind his manners:
But Beebla went on driving, till one day
A real car almost hit him at the Corner:
For safety, they took his car away.
Beebla didn't cry or throw a tantrum –
He knew that but for luck he would be dead,
And at night-time, after kisses, hugs and lights-out,
He started up his car inside his head.

Beebla got a piano once from Santa –
He ran down to the Church on Christmas Day
Before his Mammy or his Daddy could contain him
(He wanted all the crowd to hear him play).
And he walloped notes and pounded them and
    thumped them
As *Silent Night* became a noisy day,
But it was *his* noise, all his own and he could make
    it –
It said things for him that only it could say.

20

And he stole into the Church another morning
When all the crowd had scattered home
    from Mass,
And he went up to the mike like Elvis
    Presley
But he only made an echo – it was off!
So Beebla went back home to his piano,
To the sound of what it is to be alone
'Cos Beebla had no brothers or no sisters
And he often had to play all on his own.

Beebla was the crossest in the village –
He was not afraid of beast or man:
He'd jump off walls, climb trees, walk under horses –
He did it for a dare; until the Wren
When the Wren Boys dressed up in masks and
    sashes
And came into your house to dance and play –
Beebla was excited at the Wren Boys,
He simply couldn't wait for Stephen's Day;
But when the Wren Boys came to Beebla's kitchen
Like horrors that he dreaded in his dreams,
He howled, tore off into the bathroom,
And hid behind the bath and kicked and screamed.

His mother came and told him not to worry,
Brought Tom Mangan into him without the mask –
Tom Mangan was his friend, worked in the Creamery,
But today Tom Mangan caused his little heart
To pound inside his ribcage like a nightmare,
Was fear dressed up and playing for hard cash –
Tom would be his friend again tomorrow,
But today Beebla hung around the bath.

He ran away from school the day he started –
He ran before he got inside the door
And his friends who'd brought him there that
    morning
Couldn't catch him. But he'd no time to explore
The village that morning in December
Before Christmas trees were common, or lights lit –
Beebla had to figure out his problem
And he wasn't sure how he'd get out of it.

He stole into his shop and no-one noticed
(His Daddy's shop – his Mammy wasn't well)
And he hid beneath the counter till Daddy found
    him:
'Oh Daddy, Daddy, Daddy, please don't tell

Mammy that I ran from school this morning –
The doors were big and dark, the windows high;
And Dad, I ran from school this morning
– I had to – 'twas either that or cry.'
His Daddy didn't mind, his Mammy neither,
He stayed at home till Eastertime, and then
One morning he got dressed-up, took his schoolbag,
Brushed his hair, and went to school again.

He played with all the boys in *The Back Haggarts*,
A place that has no name (it's gone!) today,
High jumps, long jumps, triple jumps and marbles,
But there was one game not everyone could play –
The secret game that he was once allowed in:
Doctors where you pulled down your pants
To be examined by one who was 'The Doctor';
Beebla ran when asked to drop his pants!
And they chased him, calling him 'a coward',
But Beebla didn't want to play that fun
(Mostly 'cos a girl was 'The Doctor')
He ran in home but didn't tell anyone.

And one time, too, he fought a boy for nothing
'Cos the older boys had goaded them to fight;

After that, he never fought for nothing
'Cos he knew inside himself it wasn't right.

Beebla would annoy you with his questions –
He wanted to know everything – and why:
Why he was, what was it to be *Beebla*,
And would his mother live, or would she die?
And what was it to die? Was it like *Cowboys*
Where you could live and die and live again?
Or would Mammy be forever up in Heaven?
(Forever was how much times one-to-ten?)

This was all before the television,
About the time we got electric light,
Before bungalows, bidets or flush-toilets,
Where dark was dark, and fairies roamed the night.
This story's a true story – *honest Injun*!
You tell me that it's funny, a bit sad;
Be happy! It has a happy ending
'Cos Beebla grew up to be your Dad.

A Poem for Grandad

I made a poem for Grandad,
Most of it is true
Except for bits and pieces –
Things we used to do,

The fun we had together,
I told it like it was,
The truth of me and Grandad;
I made up bits because

Grandad's now my story,
I imagine him to be
The things we did together
And little bits of me.

I made a poem for Grandad,
Grandad's five weeks dead,
Now Grandad is the story
I see inside my head.

At the Seaside

When you paddle
In the sea
First you shiver
Then you pee
And the waves that licked your toes
Suddenly
Fizz up your nose
And you stumble
Oh the shock
And you swallow water
Yock
But it's sweaty summer weather
And it's great fun altogether

Daddy's Belly

Daddy got a belly,
It's very stickin' out
An' Mammy says he got it
From drinkin' too much stout.

Daddy's very cuddly –
He's like a teddy bear,
Safe an' soft an' spongy,
Curly kind of hair.

Daddy got a belly,
He's goin' on a diet –
Mammy said he better
An' Daddy said he try it.

Daddy got a belly
But soon he will be thinner
Drinkin' no more porter
An' eatin' lot less dinner.

My New Blue Knickers

I got new blue knickers
In a packet on a hook;
I'm wearing my new knickers –
Do you want to see them? LOOK!

I love my new blue knickers,
I'm proud as proud can be –
I can't wait to show my knickers.
EVERYBODY LOOK AT ME!

I got new blue knickers,
I'm proud as proud can be –
I'm ready, are you looking?
MY NEW BLUE KNICKERS – SEE!

A Walk in the Country

It's hard to find a toilet
When you're bursting for the loo
And you're somewhere in the country –
What are you to do?

You try to find a quiet spot
Behind a tree or ditch
But ouch! – Ah yes, a nettle
Stings you and you itch.

And if, in desperation,
You sneak into a wood,
A crow is doing his business
And it lands upon your head.

Or if in haste you disappear
Down a shady lane,
Alas! the road less travelled
Ends up in a drain;

And your socks and shoes are squelchy
And you wish you hadn't come
For a walk out in the country;
You turn around for home

'Cos it's hard to find a toilet
When you're bursting for the loo
And the countryside is treacherous
When you haven't got a clue.

MIDDLE OF
NOWHERE

Running Away

He's running away from his Mammy,
He's running away from his Dad –
He can't take any more so he's leaving;
He's snivelling, he's snuffling, he's mad.

So he goes to his room in a fury
(Making sure that his Daddy can see)
And fills up his bag with his Teddies.
But Dad just sits, cool as can be.

And he slams the front door so they'll hear him
And he sobs as he walks down the drive
And he keeps looking back towards the window
To see if the curtains are moved.

Slowly he walks down the driveway –
Oh Daddy, please call me back,
Oh Mammy, come quickly and save me,
I'm sorry now that I packed.

And he stops at the gate and he wonders
Just where do I think I am going?
And Daddy comes out and he hugs him –
It's good not to feel so alone.

'Son, where did you think you were going?
We love you, we need you, you know.'
'Oh Daddy, sure I was just bluffing.
Thanks for not letting me go.'

Confessions of a Thumb Sucker

Everyone tries to stop me,
They say that it looks dumb
But always when I'm idle
I suck my thumb.

And when everything about me
Is grumpy, gammy, glum,
When adults take out the tablets,
I suck my thumb.

My thumb is kinda dreamy
When BIGHUGE problems come
My eyes turn in and look within
As I suck my thumb.

What's a Tourist?

'Children, what's a tourist?
Can anyone tell me now?'

'Please sir, a man with a camera
Taking photos of a cow!'

Luddle-Uddle-Uddle

My baby brother has no teeth,
He can only nibble,
I can't make out a thing he says
Because he's talking scribble.

Diarrhoea

I had a queasy tummy,
I went up to the loo
And when I'd done my business
I made pooh juice instead of pooh.

And that's true.

It's Only Simple Adding

It's only simple adding,
That's all you've got to do:
Just write the sum and add it –
It's just like 2 + 2.

That's fine for you to say it,
But you have no regard –
I think that you've forgotten
When 2 + 2 was hard.

Cats

I thought cats were cuddly
Like Teddies in your bed
Until our cat brought home a mouse
And left the creature dead

On the step outside our kitchen door
And Daddy said that he
Was only trying to show us
How good a cat can be.

But the little mouse was broken,
On his nose a bead of blood,
And all this just to show us
A cat can kill real good.

He didn't want to eat him,
He just dropped him at the door,
Now I know things about cats
I didn't know before:

That no matter how you rear them
As pets in your own house,
A cat will, true to nature,
Always kill a mouse.

The True Story of Little Miss Muffet

Little Miss Muffet
Sat on a spider
(He couldn't get away) –
He went SPLAT!
She squashed him flat
And his guts came out like
    whey.

The Forty Shades of Green

In Granda's time, he told me,
They'd no toilets anywhere –
They had to do their business
In the open air

In orchards, fields and gardens
Where they would not be seen
And that's the reason, Granda says,
Why Ireland is so green.

Rain

Everyone says they hate it,
They say that it's a pain,
They say that it depresses them
But I love the rain.

I jump in puddles, splash in pools –
Rain is great for play
And the best of all about it is
It's going to rain today!

Head-Over-Heels

She loves to go head-over-heels,
She loves to go head-over-heels,
She's more often found
With her legs off the ground
'Cos she loves to go head-over-heels.

She loves to go head-over-heels,
She loves to go head-over-heels,
With her legs in the air
And her head on the chair
'Cos she loves to go head-over-heels.

She loves to go head-over-heels,
She loves to go head-over-heels,
The world, she's found,
Is as good upside-down
'Cos she loves to go head-over-heels.

She loves to go head-over-heels,
She loves to go head-over-heels,
And she looks up at you

With a different view
'Cos she loves to go head-over-heels.

Come on, let's go head-over-heels,
Come on, let's go head-over-heels,
Don't mind what they'll say,
It's great fun, let's play!
Come on, let's go head-over-heels.

Prayer

In the deepest
Dark of night
When the moon is barking
And dogs are bright
And nothing is
As nothing seems
And all my dreams
Are dreaming dreams
And I don't know
That I'm asleep
And night things howl
And prowl and creep
May I go safely
Through the deep
In the dark of night
When I'm asleep.

Amen.

I'm Proud to be Me

Though you live in a house
With a proper address
And wear proper clothes
Not my hand-me-down dress,
Though you think that you're better
Than I'll ever be
And look down on our equals,
I'm proud to be me.

I'd Like to be a Wrestler

I'd like to be a wrestler
With tree trunks for my thighs,
My hands as big as shovels,
Volcanoes for my eyes.

And if I was a wrestler
I'd be The JCB
For that's what they'd all call me.
Oh my! the things you'd see –

You'd see me lifting wrestlers
And throwing them around
And sitting down upon them
When I had them on the ground;

I'd jump on them and throw them
Out of the wrestling ring,
And when I am the champion
(Just think of it!), I'll bring

My belt back home to Mammy
And she'll be proud of me
And then she'll know her little girl
Has become The JCB.
That's me!

Splat!

It didn't come from outer space
(If it did, I wouldn't care) –
Oh no! It was much worse than that
When a bird pooped on my hair.

I was minding my own business
Playing in the yard
When I felt this plop upon my head
Catching me off guard.

When I reached up to investigate,
I felt this sticky goo,
And all my friends were laughing
That my hair was stuck with pooh;

And then I started crying –
I cried most bitterly
That of all the places that pooh could land
It had to land on me.

And I wouldn't let them wash me –
Oh Lord! It wasn't fair
So I just sat and sulked and sobbed
That a bird pooped on my hair.
I just sat and sulked and sobbed
That a bird pooped on my hair.

When Tommy Fell into the Bin

The Infants were out in the toilets
And whatever way Tommy came in
(How did he manage to do it?),
Tommy fell into the bin.

I don't know how he managed to do it –
He was walking quite normally in
Drying his hands with a tissue
When Tommy fell into the bin.

He fell in like a sack of potatoes
And everyone saw him fall in –
It took Mrs Strong to extract him
When Tommy fell into the bin.

He fell in like a sack of potatoes
And only that Tommy is thin
He'd be stuck down inside there forever
When Tommy fell into the bin.

He would.
When Tommy fell into the bin.

An Answer to my Prayer

Mammy died a year ago
And I was only five;
Daddy and I wanted
Mam to be alive

But she's alive in heaven,
I talk to her at night
Because I say my prayers to her
That we will be all right.

And suddenly this morning
I woke up at dawn,
I hopped into Daddy's bed,
He woke up with a yawn.

I said 'Good morning, Daddy,
Let's have a cup of tea',
We went into the kitchen
And he made tea for me.

We drank our tea together
Myself and Dad,

Just to be beside him
Made me glad

And as the morning brightened
And although we had been sad
I hugged and kissed my dad and said
'Aren't we very happy, Dad?'

Shopping with Mammy

Shopping with Mammy
Is a definite no,
She may have been cool
But 'twas long, long ago,

For the things that she says
Would look good on me
I just couldn't bear
My buddies to see;

It even makes uniforms
Not look so bad –
Next time, I think,
I'll go shopping with Dad

For he doesn't care
Whatever I pick,
No, he doesn't care
Just as long as I'm quick

But shopping with Mammy
Is a definite pain,
I'll never go shopping
With Mammy again.

(Until the next time.)

When you make a Smelly

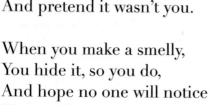

When you make a smelly,
What are you to do?
You act like all the others
And pretend it wasn't you.

When you make a smelly,
You hide it, so you do,
And hope no one will notice
The smelly came from you.

You do!

A Hug

A hug is huge and happy,
It warms you through and through –
Even when you're lonely,
It makes you good as new.

A hug is huge and happy,
A hug is what you do
When you open up from inside out
And let your feelings through.

A hug is huge and happy,
A hug is always true –
It's just pretend when it's not
    meant
'Cos a hug makes one of two.

Basher

Basher is a bully,
He thumps me, calls me names,
Always wants to be the boss
At lessons and at games.

Basher is a bully,
I get headaches, so I do,
I get headaches every morning
Before I go to school

'Cos Basher always bullies me
And makes my life so hard
But I can't keep away from him
In class or in the yard;

No, I can't keep away from him
Although I know I should
And every time I play with him
It turns out no good.

No, I can't keep away from him
No matter how I try
'Cos I want him to notice me.
That's why.

I want him to notice me
And, when he does, it's great
But mostly it's being bullied
And these headaches that I hate.

Mostly it's being bullied
In class and out at play.
I'll have to tell the teacher
And learn to keep away.

I'll have to tell the teacher
And learn to keep away.

I will.

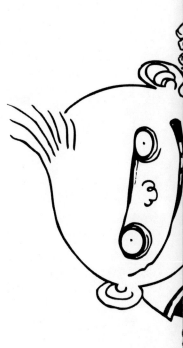

A Boy and His Dog

He played with me, I slept on him
Those summers in the sun
But now my dog is dying
And we have to put him down.

He played with me when I was young,
He was my greatest friend
But now he's blind and dying.
This is the end.

Goodbye, old friend, I'll miss you,
We'll put you out of pain
But I know I'll never, ever see
The likes of you again.

Goodbye, old friend, I'll miss you
My childhood ends today,
The summers that I slept on you,
The games we used to play.

Goodbye, goodbye, dear Sandy,
I'll hold you to the end
I'd swap all other dogs for you,
My bestest, bestest friend.

Popularity

I don't mind if I'm not popular,
Not if I have to do
Things that I don't want to
Now I've thought it through.

I don't mind if I'm not popular,
Let the others laugh at me,
I don't think that it's important,
And popularity

Is for the ones who tease me
(They tease so they can show
Their friends that they don't want me);
Does it hurt me? No!

Although once it used to
And I wondered why,
But now I know I'm different
To the other girls and boys.

Yes, now I know I'm different
But that's OK by me,
I've learned to accept myself,
And popularity

Is fine for those who need it
But I don't now that I
Accept that I'm different
And no longer wonder why.

It's fine for those who need it
But I don't now that I
Accept that I'm different
And no longer wonder why.

It's OK.

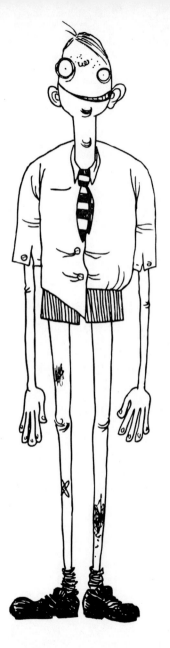

Bored

Don't want to do no lessons,
Don't really want to play,
Sitting on the wall here,
It's a boring day.

Sitting with my friends here
Bored as bored can be
And it's no consolation
That they're as bored as me.

Sitting with my friends here
On this boring wall,
Watching all the younger kids
Running, playing ball.

Sitting on the wall here
While all the others play,
Nothing to do and all day to do it,
It's a BORING day.

How High?

How high can I piddle?
Higher than the door?
But the piddle hit it halfways up
And dribbled on the floor.

I got a ball of tissue
And rubbed the floor till dry
And soaked it off the lino.
Wow! I can piddle high!

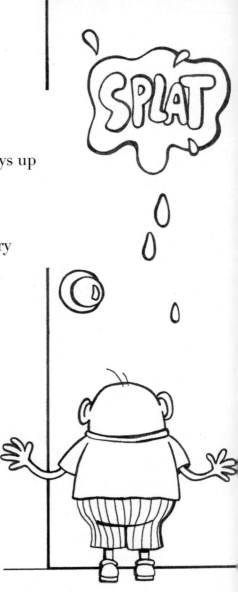

Learning the Tin Whistle

I'm learning the tin whistle –
I play it really fast,
But the tune just runs away from me
(In this race, I'm always last).

The more the tune runs onwards,
The faster I must play
Till I run out of fingers
And the tune gets clean away.

Come back Peg Ryan's Polka,
The Dawning of the Day,
The Britches Full of Stitches,
Come back and let me play.

I'll play you soft and easy,
I'll practise day and night –
Oh please slow down and wait for me
Till the music comes out right.

I'll play you soft and easy
Till feet tap on the ground
And all the air is music
In my cylinder of sound.

Come back Peg Ryan's Polka,
Give me one more chance –
My notes will turn to music
When my fingers learn to dance.

The Moving Stair

The first time I went to Limerick
We went into this big store,
They had tons of things for grown-ups
On the bottom floor.

And Mammy went to sample
All sorts of perfume there
When, just below the counter,
I saw this moving stair.

So I jumped upon it
With a spaceman kind of hop
And up, up, up I floated
But the stair just wouldn't stop.

And then when I had gotten up
I felt a proper clown
For the stair just kept on moving –
How was I to get down?

And then it dawned upon me
That I was alone and lost
And I was small and frightened
And Mammy would be cross.

So then, I suppose you've guessed it,
I let out such a roar
That Mammy dropped the perfume
Down on the bottom floor;

And Mammy – she came for me
And I wasn't lost at all
But that was quite a while ago
When I was young and small.

A Goodnight Kiss

I pulled my sister's hair,
I hit her with my shoe,
Daddy's very mad at me –
I know what he'll do:

No story when it's bedtime,
A kiss will have to do
For, though he's very mad at me,
Dad loves bold boys too.

Now we are Eight

Dad, they called you "Gabriel",
Dad, I wonder why –
"Gabriel"'s such a big name
For such a little boy.

Did they always call you "Gabriel",
Dad, when you were small?
Or did your name get bigger
As you grew up? Do all

Our names get bigger, Dad,
When we grow up? You see
I'm not too sure when I grow up
That "Nessa" will fit me.

Grandad

When people think of grandads,
They think of rocking chairs
And woolly rugs and slippers
And baldy wisps of hair.

That wasn't like my grandad,
He always seemed so young –
Though he was eighty years and more,
He loved to mix among

People who were younger,
He never acted old
And you knew he'd always love you
Even when you were bold.

Yes! Grandad was as young as me
In many, many ways,
And now he's dead, I think of him
And all the nights and days

He minded me and made me feel
Just like a small boy should
For life with him was happy,
And life, like him, was good.

Number Two

When you're going to the toilet
And you make your number two
(Perhaps I should explain here –
That's what I call pooh),

And no matter how you flush it
You can't sink it like a boat
(Sometimes it's unsinkable,
A pooh that's meant to float),

And it sits there on the water
Daring you to try
Till you cover it with papers
And hope no-one will spy

You as you sneak out
Defeated by the pooh,
You pray no-one will notice
This turd was made by you.

Peace

Just to sit here with my rabbit
As evening gently falls
With rustling in the hedges
And roses on the walls;
Just to sit here in the evening,
My rabbit on my chest,
A late bee in the fuchsia
Is the time that I love best.

Just to sit here in the garden
And watch my rabbit hop
From tree to bush to flower
Then suddenly to stop
And listen to the evening
And smell, her nose a-twitch,
Is all I need of heaven.
Such evenings I am rich.

Do Teachers Fart?

Do teachers fart?
What do you think?
I stood beside one,
Smelled the stink.

But I don't think
A teacher would –
Aren't teachers always
Very good?

Do teachers fart?
I just can't tell
But if teacher didn't
Who made the smell?

Who?

Tomato Sandwiches

Soggy tomato sandwiches
Are the ones that I like best –
You can keep your biscuits,
Crackers and the rest.

I make them in the morning
Before I go to school
And when I've finished making them
I soak them in the pool

Of tomato juice upon the plate
So they go soft and pink –
They're soggy and they're juicy!
I really really think

That there's nothing in this world as nice
As a sandwich made this way –
And the best of all about it is
I'm having some today.

Her First Flight

'I love you, Dad! I love you!
I love this massive plane –
It looks like a big fat pencil-case
(Aer Spain – is it, Dad? Aer Spain?).

This aeroplane's exciting,
It's noise-ing up to go –
Will it drive as fast as you, Dad?
But, Dad, we're going slow.'

'We're driving to our runway, dear,
And then we'll go real fast –
Faster than even I drive.'
'Whee, Dad! Whee! At last!

We're going really speedy,
When are we going to fly?
Wow! Up, up, up we go, Dad!
'Way up in the sky.

What's happening to my ears, Dad?
They're funny – I can't hear
(Well, kind of) what you say, Dad?
There's something in my ears.'

'Suck a sweet, 'twill help you –
It's a good idea.'
'Who's Eddie, Dad? Eddie?'
'I said it's a good *idea*.

Look at the clouds now, Nessa,
We're coming to them – just;
In a minute we'll be through them.'
'Dad, it's like they're made of dust –

The clouds are awful dusty,
I can't see a thing –
Just dark outside my window.
Now what's happening?

We're above the clouds! The sunshine!'
'Sit back now and relax.
It's three hours to Tenerife –
Let's have a little nap.'

'Daddy, we're not moving –
Look down at the sea:
It's not moving, we're not moving;
This is boring – I have my wee.

Daddy, where's the toilet?
I'm bored with this oul' plane.'
'Look out the window, Nessa –
Look down and you'll see Spain.'

'Daddy, where's the toilet?
Is there any on this plane?'
'OK, OK, I'll take you;'
'Daddy, we're over Spain …

When I was at the toilet,
I made poops as well as wee –
Where did the poops go, Daddy?
The poops I made, the wee?

Did they fall down on some Spanish man
'Way 'way down below?
Where did my poops go, Daddy?
Where did my wee-wee go?

What's next after Spain, Dad?
Will we get our dinner soon?
This aeroplane's exciting.
How far up is the moon?

Dad, my ears are popping –
Is everything all right?
Daddy, oops! I chewed my sweet
I got such an awful fright.

But it's OK now, Daddy –
It's just the plane going down.
Daddy, Daddy! Tenner Reef!
Dad, is this our town?'

My Puppy Charlie

My puppy Charlie,
He bites and he bites,
He bites fingers and papers
And curtains and tights;

He barks all night long
And he messes the place
But he's furry and cuddly
And he licks my face.

Blossoming

Little buds upon a tree
Blossom forth eventually
Like me

First they open then they bloom
Pushing out to make more room
Like me

And they flower as they please
And their beauty feeds the bees
Like me

Yes the blossoms flower and fruit
Growing into their own truth
Like me

Thank you God for me

The Part of Mary in the Christmas Play

I got the part of Mary
In the Christmas play –
'Twas grand until I realised
I had no lines to say.

First the Angel came to me –
I had to bow my head
And look as sickly sweet as pie.
I wish I'd lines instead.

Then I had to follow Joseph –
I had no lines to say
(Even the two dressed as the donkey
Got to bray);

But I had to follow Joseph
Quiet as a mouse
While he went from inn to inn
And house to boarding house.

Then I had to hold the baby
When the shepherds came to pray;
And the same again for the Wise Men.
I wish I'd lines to say.

Don't you think that Mary
Would get to say a word;
After all, 'twas she that chose –
The mother of the Lord!

Don't you think that such a woman
Would have more to do
Than look as sickly sweet as pie
Forever dressed in blue?

Don't you think that such a woman
Should have lines to say
Instead of being an extra
In the Christmas play?

Saturday Night

Rub-a-dub-dub
Look what's in the tub!
Little Boy Blue with his horn,
Little Bo Peep
Who's lost all her sheep
(No wonder she looks so forlorn);

Little Jack Horner
In from the corner,
Little Miss Muffet's there too –
It's Saturday night
And they're scrubbed till they're bright
By the Woman who Lives in the Shoe.

My Dog

His tongue hangs out when he is hot
And when he runs you see his bottom,
His tail straight up and waving 'round,
His four feet hardly touch the ground
As he runs before us up the drive
Barking, glad to be alive,
So excited he does his wee,
I love him and he loves me.
My dog.

Bursting Pimples

Did you ever burst a pimple?
It doesn't hurt at all –
The white stuff shoots right out of it
To the mirror on the wall;

And then you get a tissue
To mop up bits of blood
And you flush it down the toilet
And it goes off with the flood.

And you polish up the mirror
To get rid of all the goo
And you flush that down the toilet
Too.

Oh I love bursting pimples!
It doesn't hurt at all
When all the bad inside you
Is splattered on the wall.

Imagination

Imagination is the thing that
Makes you magic
And
Gives you
Inspiration to make everything
New,
And
To
Invent things that are
Only seen by you, where
Nothing is impossible. Imagine!

In Summer

Just me and my friend Jessie
Sitting on the grass;
All the sun-long summer
We watch the world pass.

Just me and my friend Jessie
Sitting real slow
On the ditch outside our driveway
With the radio.

We listen to it sometimes
But mostly we just laze
And listen to the buzzing
And flutter of the days.

The lazy days, the hazy days
We hope will never end
Just sitting on the roadside,
Me and my best friend.

In summer.

Love Your Bum

'Love your bum', the slogan said.
Ugh! The thought of it –
An ad for toilet paper, I thought
This is pushing things a bit.

But then I got to thinking
It's good; no matter what,
Love is good for everything,
Even for you bot.

So love your bum. Believe me,
If you love like that, you'll find
That you can love most anything.
Even your behind.

Love your bum!

To:
My Bum

Love

Terry Turner in my class
Is cute as cute can be,
I'd love to sit beside him
So he could talk to me.

But he won't sit beside me,
No matter how I try
He never wants to talk to me –
He only talks to boys.

And so today I kicked him,
I kicked him on the knee,
He thumped me hard for kicking him
But at least he noticed me.

He thumped me hard for kicking him
But at least he noticed me.

He did!

My Best Friend

My best friend was Grandad.
I used to stay at his house on Friday nights
And that was great fun.
He used to take me to the chipper
After the nine o'clock news
And he'd buy two cartons of curried chips and two
  sausages
And we'd eat them in his kitchen during *The Late
  Late Show*.
He used to come up to our house on Sundays for
  dinner
And I'd always want to sit beside him at the table.

I remember one Christmas I had just got a snooker
  table.
Grandad came up for Christmas dinner
And I had asked everybody else to play with me.
They all said no, they were too busy.
Grandad was in the middle of setting the table
And I asked him to play and he said he would.
He came over

And I actually had to place the balls for him
It was so long since he had played snooker!

Well Grandad was my best friend;
He was so kind.
He was just unique to me.
Like he didn't know much Irish
Because when he was young he hadn't much time
    for school
(He had to help at home on the farm, he said,
And at fourteen years had to hire himself with farmers
Because he had thirteen brothers and sisters
And times were bad)
But I often did my Irish homework with him and
    he always ended up right.

I remember the day Grandad died.
It was March.
I can't remember the date.
He rang Mom and said he thought he was having a
    heart attack.
We rushed down to his house –
We got there in two and a half minutes
And when we went in we found Grandad lying on
    the floor moaning.

And then he just died.
And I was below in the room crying
And then Mom and Nessa and Dad started crying
    too.

At the Funeral Parlour I forgot myself
And said 'I'm sitting beside Grandad.'
But Grandad was in his coffin.

He was dead.

It was fine until they closed the coffin
And then I knew I'd never see him again in this life.

Goodbye, Grandad, my best friend.
Goodbye
Goodbye.